IRELAND TRAVEL GUIDE 2023

The Most Complete Pocket Guide to Discover Ireland | Everything you Need to Know about the History, Art, Food and Folklore of the Emerald Isle

BY

MIKE J. DARCEY

© Copyright 2023 - All rights reserved.

It is not legal to reproduce, duplicate, or transmit any part of this document in either electronic means or printed format. Recording of this publication is strictly prohibited and any storage of this document is not allowed unless with written permission from the publisher except for the use of brief quotations in a book review.

Table of Contents

INTRODUCTION 6

CHAPTER 1. THE HISTORICAL OVERVIEW OF IRELAND 10

    CULTURAL HERITAGE ART AND ARCHITECTURE 14

CHAPTER 1.   IRELAND ITINERARIES 15

    SIGHTSEEING SITES IN IRELAND 18

    SAFETY TO VISIT THE SITES 20

    MISTAKES TO AVOID AND SAVE TIME AND MONEY WHILE TRAVELING IN IRELAND 24

CHAPTER 2 THE IRELAND'S TOP ATTRACTIONS 28

    DUBLIN CITY 28

    COASTAL RING OF KERRY 28

    CONNEMARA REGION 29

    BLARNEY STONE FORTRESS 30

    GIANT'S CAUSEWAY 31

    KYLEMORE CASTLE 32

    THE NATIONAL MUSEUM OF IRELAND 33

    CORK CITY 34

    ST. PATRICK'S CATHEDRAL 35

    KILLARNEY NATIONAL PARK 36

    THE GUINNESS STOREHOUSE 37

    THE CLIFFS OF MOHER 38

    GLENDALOUGH 39

CHAPTER 3. THE"HIDDEN GEMS" OF IRELAND 41

    DINGLE 41

    INCH 43

    KINSALE 44

Murphy's Ice Cream Parlour 45

Kerry International Dark-Sky Reserve 46

CHAPTER 4. THE LOCAL CULTURE OF IRELAND 48

Tips for avoiding crowds 52

Ireland's best restaurants, clubs and nightlife .. 56

List of typical Irish foods and drinks to try on a trip to Ireland 62

CHAPTER 5. THE BEST PLACES TO STAY 67

Hotels: 68

Airbnb: 68

CHAPTER 6. ACTIVITIES 70

1. Go on a picnic 70

2. Visit the library 72

3. Attend a community concert 73

4. Visit a beach 75

5. Visit a lighthouse 76

6. Go on a nature hike 78

CHAPTER 7. TRANSPORTATION 80

Taxi 80

Bus 81

Cycling 82

Tram 82

Train 83

Maps of attractions 85

CHAPTER 8. SEASONS TO TRAVEL 91

Packing 92

Spring 93

Summer 93

Winter 94

Autumn..94

CHAPTER 9. THE CURRENCY EXCHANGE 96

1. Check the Rates Online..97

2. Use a Credit Card..98

3. Pay in the Local Currency 99

CHAPTER 10. IRISH DIALECT EXPRESSIONS 100

Introduction

Ireland is a beautiful and historic country, famous for its stunning landscapes. You'll find everything from lush green cliffs to snow-capped mountains and charming fishing villages.

To make the most of your visit to Ireland, you'll need to decide what kind of experiences you want to have. The best times to visit are spring, summer or fall, but winter can be a nice time too, especially if you enjoy being out and about in the great outdoors.

Climate

Despite being situated in the temperate latitudes of western Europe, Ireland's climate is not uniform and can be very variable. The influence of the Atlantic Gulf Stream is a major factor in the weather, meaning that summers can be warm and rainy, while winters are cool and dry.

The climatic conditions vary greatly by region, with the inland areas being generally cooler in winter and warmer in summer than coastal areas. Nevertheless, the coastal regions tend to be the most popular areas of the country to visit in the summer and autumn periods due to the pleasant temperatures they enjoy.

In general, rainfall is widespread and tends to be heaviest along the west coast. In particular, if you're visiting the Wild Atlantic Way coastline or taking a beach holiday in Northern Ireland, you may want to pack a waterproof jacket in case there are any downpours during your stay.

Summer in Ireland can be pleasantly warm, with average temperatures reaching around 16 degC (61 degF). If you're planning on swimming or surfing at the beaches along the Wild Atlantic Way coastal drive, it's a good idea to pack a beach towel and a waterproof suit.

However, summer in Ireland is also characterized by periods of very hot weather with temperatures reaching highs of 27 degC (80.5 degF) on Malin Head on the north coast and 29 degC (85 degF) in a Dublin park.

In winter, the climate is chilly but rarely freezing, with snowfall a very rare occurrence. It's also possible to experience milder winters in the inland parts of the country, due to the influence of the Gulf Stream.

Language

The Irish language (also known as Gaelic) is one of the most important parts of Ireland's culture and history. The country's language heritage is rooted in the traditions of traditional literature, mythology and folklore that date back thousands of years. The literary tradition has survived to a degree not seen in other European languages and today, Irish is taught as a subject in many university degrees worldwide.

The language is a Goidelic language of the Insular Celtic branch of the Celts and is closely related to Welsh (Cymraeg), Cornish (Kernewek) and Breton (Brezhoneg). Its grammatical structure is similar to other members of this family.

In addition to the two ways of expressing this verb, there are also a number of other grammatical differences between dialects of the language. For instance, ni is often used instead of cha(n) when talking about negative things, though cha(n) has become more widespread in recent decades.

Another characteristic of Irish grammar is that it has both conjunctive and disjunctive forms for pronouns. These are used to emphasize a personal pronoun, or to form passives when a subject pronoun is missing from the sentence. The numbers can be either human or non-human, and are usually in a disjunctive form.

It's always helpful to have a basic knowledge of the language before you visit Ireland, especially if you plan to travel to Gaeltacht areas, where a lot of people still speak in Irish.

Customs

Having a good understanding of the customs in Ireland is important when traveling to this country. This will help you interact with local people smoothly and avoid awkward situations during your trip.

The customs in Ireland vary between different regions and ethnic groups. For example, some Christian denominations have their own traditions while others are shared with other countries around the world.

One of the Irish customs that you should be aware of before you visit is that they value conversations and enjoy engaging in them. If you are visiting them for the first time, it is best to be sociable and talk to them about anything they want without getting into any arguments.

It is also considered a tradition for Irish people to speak about the weather forecast when meeting each other. This is especially true for those who have just arrived to the country as they may not be familiar with the weather in the area.

Another important aspect to know about etiquette in Ireland is that you should never smoke in public places. To give a good impression, it is recommended that you offer a firm handshake and maintain eye contact when greeting people in Ireland. These can be flowers or a bottle of wine, among other things. These can be given as a token of appreciation for the hospitality you've received during your stay in Ireland.

Transportation

Ireland is a small island that relies heavily on public transport. Getting around on foot or by bus, tram or train is a great way to explore the city centers and rural regions. If you want to see the best of the country, though, it's a good idea to bring your own car or hire one while you're here.

This prepaid ticket works on the rail and bus systems in Dublin, Cork and Galway and is hugely convenient for tourists. It saves you an average of twenty percent on your journey.

However, they are expensive compared to other means of transportation, and it's important to ensure you are getting a licensed driver. You can use a taxi-fare estimator on the Transport for Ireland website to get an idea of how much your taxi ride will cost.

You can also rent a car in Ireland, although this is not as widely available as it is in other European countries. You can find rentals at major airports and on the mainland. You can also hire a private driver for a tour of Ireland, but be prepared to pay a lot of money for this service.

Chapter 1.
The historical overview of Ireland.

Ireland has a long and varied history that continues to influence its culture today. That history is represented not only in the townscapes and cityscapes but also throughout the landscape in the form of countless archaeological and historical monuments.

History

Ireland is a small island country that is famous for many things including its culture, art, music and drink. It has a long history that is filled with many different stories.

Thousands of years ago, Ireland was an uninhabited wilderness. In the 17th century Ireland became part of the United Kingdom. This led to many issues such as the Great Famine of 1845 and emigration from Ireland to the United States.

The Irish landscape is filled with archaeology and history, revealing the country's long, fascinating history. It was home to people with bronze tools and weapons, who erected stone circles and crannogs (lake dwellings) in the early Bronze Age. These were followed by the arrival of the Celts in 500 BC, who brought iron tools and weapons. They were a warlike people, so they built strong forts to defend their areas.

During this time, Christianity is introduced to Ireland in AD 432, opening the way for a new religion and a new way of life. This is when the first churches are built, the Book of Kells is created and Irish literature starts to develop in Latin and Gaelic.

The development of the modern Irish economy and society is accompanied by the growth of an art industry that is both strong and vibrant. This includes the film and animation industries, which have won critical acclaim internationally. In performance arts, there are a number of theatres around the country. The country also has a large music scene, with the national symphony and the Dublin Philharmonic Orchestra among its most famous performers.

Ireland has an exceptionally long history of art. Its culture has been shaped by art over the millennia, and much of its artistic heritage is preserved in the country's museums.

The country's history is also marked by its architecture. Ireland's buildings are a visual record of its turbulent past, as well as the roots of its agrarian economy.

Thousands of castles and forts line the countryside. They were constructed in the form of stone circles and crannogs (lake dwellings).

After that, the Celts arrived, brought with them iron tools and weapons. They were a warlike people, and warfare between them was frequent.

Many of Ireland's towns and cities are still based on the ancient settlements that were once a part of this landscape. They have become UNESCO World Heritage Sites.

As a result, these historic buildings and sites have been protected from destruction by the government. They are now cherished and respected by the people of Ireland, and are often used as symbols for national identity.

The Irish Historic Towns Atlases (IHTA) is a groundbreaking, multi-volume series that traces the development of towns and cities across Ireland. It is the first comprehensive study of its kind and is published by Yale University Press with funding from the Naughton Foundation, the Irish Ministry of Arts, Heritage and Gaeltacht, and the Mellon Centre for Studies in British Art.

Music

Ireland is known for its vibrant cultural landscape, combining modern trends with its own rich history. It is home to a long tradition of literature, including the work of some of the world's most prominent writers such as Joyce, Wilde and Beckett. It also has a thriving musical tradition that is well represented in popular music.

Circa 500 BC-432: The Iron Age sees the emergence of a unique Irish culture that develops language, religion and material culture. During this time, Ireland became a seafaring people who established colonies in Scotland, Wales and England as well as along river arteries of continental Europe.

From 500 to 800, the Golden Age of Early Christian Ireland was a period of remarkable learning and the arts. Many monasteries were founded throughout the island and monks kept Greek-Roman learning alive while also producing illuminated manuscripts that were an integral part of early Irish art and literature.

During the Dark Ages, Irish monks continued to keep Graeco-Roman learning alive while creating elaborate metalwork and illuminated manuscripts. This era also saw the arrival of Christianity in Ireland, which radically changed Irish politics and culture.

The early 19th century saw a resurgence of interest in Irish traditional music, which spread across Europe and to the United States. In the 1960s, elements of this tradition were embraced by rock musicians to create a distinctive Irish popular music form with international appeal.

Literature

Literature in Ireland has a long and rich history. Irish writing is one of the oldest traditions in Western culture, with the earliest Gaelic manuscripts dating back to the 4th century and preserving a large body of folklore, genealogies and poetry.

During the Middle Ages, literary societies were essential in Irish society. They carried down traditional traditions, acted as repositories of lore and genealogy, and doubled as maps. In addition, satire was an integral part of Irish literature. It often played an assassination role.

The twentieth century saw many famous writers from Ireland. Some authors, such as Caitlin Maude and Nuala Ni Dhomhnaill, are conscious of tradition but modernist in outlook. Others, such as Patrick Kavanagh, wrote about the small farmer's and shopkeeper's world of their day.

Prehistoric monuments - such as the Neolithic passage tombs of Knowth and Newgrange - are testament to the country's rich heritage. Other historic sites, like Bru na Boinne, give visitors a glimpse into ancient civilizations, royal histories, and more.

The arrival of the Celts (also known as Gaels) is also a major event in the country's history. This era is marked by the introduction of bronze tools and weapons, permanent settlement, agriculture, animal husbandry, and the development of polished stone tools and artifacts.

In AD 432, Saint Patrick introduced Christianity to Ireland. This religious change ushered in a period of significant cultural development, as the monasteries became centers of learning, knowledge production and art.

During this time, the island's secluded location also provided a safe haven for European scholars fleeing the continent. The result is a sophisticated monastic culture with a tradition of illuminated manuscripts.

The end of the Celtic Age marks the beginning of the Iron Age, which is characterised by a widespread system of feudalism and castles. In the Anglo-Norman invasion of

Ireland, the king of England sends his troops to take over large areas and restructure the country's social structure.

Cultural heritage art and architecture

In Ireland, tradition and heritage play a vital role in people's lives. They're passed down from generation to generation through music, dance and storytelling.

Many Irish traditions are still a part of daily life today, including the Celtic calendar and religious rituals. For instance, the ancient festival of Imbolc heralds spring; Bealtaine celebrates summer; Lughnasadh heralds autumn; and Samhain heralds winter.

These customs have a deep meaning in Irish culture, which is rooted in traditional pagan beliefs and values. Catholicism was the prevailing religion in Ireland in years gone by, but it has become less important in recent times.

Despite the fact that many Irish are non-Christian, a strong sense of faith is still present. You can see this in the religious bells that are rung each evening as a call to prayer for Catholics.

Another great place to visit is the EPIC museum in Belfast, where you can explore the stories of 10 ten million people who have left Ireland for various reasons over the centuries. From famine to conflict to religious persecution, these immigrants brought their culture with them and created a new one abroad.

Chapter 2.
Ireland Itineraries

It has plenty of things to offer, including stunning landscapes, castles, historic sites, lively cities, and of course, the famous Irish pubs.

- Dublin and the East Coast: If you're short on time, this itinerary is perfect as it focuses on Dublin and the surrounding area. Spend a few days exploring the vibrant city of Dublin, including the Guinness Storehouse, Trinity College, and the Temple Bar area. Then, take a day trip to the stunning Wicklow Mountains National Park or visit the ancient ruins of Newgrange and Knowth.
- Castles and History: Start in Dublin and visit the famous Dublin Castle before heading south to the historic city of Kilkenny.
- Northern Ireland: This itinerary covers the northern part of the island, including Belfast and the stunning Causeway Coast. Start in Belfast and visit the Titanic Museum before heading north to the Giant's Causeway and the Carrick-a-Rede rope bridge.

No matter which one you choose, you're sure to have a memorable trip filled with stunning landscapes, friendly locals, and plenty of craic (fun).

Dublin and the East Coast (5 Days)

Day 1: Arrive in Dublin and spend the day exploring the city.

Day 2: Take a day trip to the Wicklow Mountains National Park. Visit the stunning Powerscourt Estate and Gardens, and hike to the top of Sugarloaf Mountain for breathtaking views.

Day 3: Explore the city's museums, such as the National Museum of Ireland or the Irish Museum of Modern Art.

Day 4: Take a day trip to the ancient ruins of Newgrange and Knowth, dating back to 3200 BC. Alternatively, explore the historic town of Kilkenny.

Day 5: On your last day, visit the fishing village of Howth, located just north of Dublin. Take a cliff walk for stunning views, visit the Howth Castle and Gardens, and enjoy fresh seafood for lunch before departing.

The Wild Atlantic Way (10 Days)

Day 1-3: Start in Galway and explore the city's vibrant music scene and historic sites, such as the Galway Cathedral and Eyre Square.

Day 4-5: Drive to the Cliffs of Moher for breathtaking views, and then head south to the charming town of Dingle. Explore the Dingle Peninsula, including the stunning Slea Head Drive and the Gallarus Oratory.

Day 6-7: Head further south to Killarney, where you can explore the Ring of Kerry and Killarney National Park.

Day 8-10: Continue along the Wild Atlantic Way to Cork, stopping at the charming towns of Kenmare and Kinsale along the way. Visit the Jameson Distillery and the historic Blarney Castle before departing.

Castles and History (7 Days)

Day 1: Arrive in Dublin and visit Dublin Castle, St. Patrick's Cathedral, and Trinity College.

Day 2: Drive to the historic city of Kilkenny and visit the Kilkenny Castle and the medieval St. Canice's Cathedral.

Day 3-4: Head south to the stunning Rock of Cashel, a medieval castle perched on a hilltop.

Day 5-6: Drive north to the historic town of Limerick, and visit the medieval Bunratty Castle and Folk Park.

Day 7: Return to Dublin, stopping at the ancient ruins of Newgrange and Knowth on the way.

Northern Ireland (5 Days)

Day 1-2: Start in Belfast and visit the Titanic Museum and the historic Crumlin Road Gaol. Explore the city's vibrant music scene and visit the Belfast Castle.

Day 3-4: Drive to the stunning Causeway Coast, and visit the Giant's Causeway and the Carrick-a-Rede rope bridge.

Explore the walled city of Derry and learn about its history.

Day 5: Return to Belfast, stopping at the Dark Hedges and other Game of Thrones filming locations along the way.

Sightseeing Sites in Ireland

The Rock of Cashel - This historic site in County Tipperary features a medieval castle perched on a hilltop, along with a 12th-century round tower and a Romanesque chapel.

Dublin Castle - This historic castle in the heart of Dublin has been a symbol of English rule in Ireland for centuries. You can take a tour of the castle and see the State Apartments, the Chapel Royal, and the Dubhlinn Gardens.

Blarney Castle - This medieval castle in County Cork is famous for its Blarney Stone, which legend has it gives the gift of the gab to those who kiss it.

Kylemore Abbey - This beautiful Benedictine monastery in County Galway is set on the shores of a tranquil lake and surrounded by mountains. You can explore the gardens and take a tour of the castle.

Kilmainham Gaol - This former prison in Dublin played a significant role in Irish history, and many of the leaders of the 1916 Easter Rising were imprisoned here.

Safety to visit the sites

If you are planning a trip to Ireland, then you will want to make sure that you take all the necessary precautions to ensure your safety. While Ireland is one of Europe's safest countries, there are still things you need to know about travel safety in Ireland.

Theft, burglary and purse snatching are common in tourist areas especially when it's busy, so be aware of your belongings at all times. Use a fanny pack or security wallet to keep your passports, money and other valuables secure.

Spring and Summer

If you're thinking about going sightseeing in Ireland, the weather is a big factor. It's worth weighing up the pros and cons of each season to determine which is best for your particular itinerary.

The 'Peak' Season (mid-June through early September) is ideal for visitors who want to take advantage of long days and sunshine. It's also the time to experience some of the country's most famous sights and attractions, including Dublin's Trinity College and Book of Kells and the famous Blarney Castle in County Cork.

High season, however, also means higher airfares and accommodation prices. Fortunately, travel during the "Shoulder Season" offers a compromise: fewer crowds, less competition for rooms and all the tourist fun without the extra expense.

June and July have the least rainfall of any month, making this a great time for hiking and exploring Ireland's countryside. This is also the best time to see some of Ireland's most scenic beaches, from Inch Strand in County Kerry to Portrush in Northern Ireland.

If you're not a beach bum, the 'Shoulder Season' is still a good time to visit some of the country's most impressive castles and monasteries or explore the lush green countryside. In fact, the Wild Atlantic Way and Sliabh Liag cliffs are especially popular with travelers in these months, so it's a good idea to plan your trip around these attractions.

Autumn is another ideal time for exploring Ireland's natural environment. The cliffs and parks of the southwest are particularly stunning, while the golden beaches of Wexford in the southeast offer an escape from civilization.

Those who love walking will find plenty of trails to choose from, and you can easily find routes that suit any level of fitness or experience. Those who are more interested in history will love the ancient castles, monasteries and Georgian mansions found throughout Ireland.

The gray skies of an Irish winter can be loved by photographers, but they are also accompanied by weeks of rain that can make the countryside uninviting. But if you're looking for an Irish city break, the dreary days of December through February are also a great time to explore Belfast, Dublin or Cork.

Fall

A fall is a serious injury and can be dangerousIf you can do this, you can reduce the risk of a fall or take action to remove them altogether.

You can do this by using a combination of methods, including taking a multifactorial assessment or attending a falls prevention programme. This can be a great way to help you to stay safe in the long run, especially if you are elderly.

Another option is to take part in a falls prevention exercise program, led by an occupational therapist. This can help you to strengthen your muscles and improve your balance.

You can find more information about fall safety in the Irish health system on the website for the National Integrated Care Programme for Older People (NICP). The NIPCP was developed to improve the quality of life for older people and their carers and to ensure that health care services are providing optimal levels of care for their needs.

While falls are a common occurrence, they can be prevented. It's important to do this because they are very serious and can put a strain on the health system. In fact, in the United States alone, falls account for a substantial number of hospital admissions and have an impact on overall quality of life. The majority of falls occur at home and in public places, so it's important to be aware of the dangers and what you can do to keep yourself safe.

Winter

When it comes to going sightseeing in Ireland, it's important to know when it's best to go so you can plan your itinerary accordingly. There are many factors that go into choosing the right time of year for a visit to Ireland, including your personal preferences and what you want to see on your trip.

Another advantage of traveling during this time is that you'll find that hotels and accommodations are generally cheaper. You'll be able to save some money on your vacation while still having plenty of time to enjoy the beautiful Irish landscape.

However, it's important to note that the weather can be unpredictable and you should never travel without checking the weather forecast. This will help you to ensure that you pack the proper clothing and equipment for your trip.

One of the most essential items you should pack when visiting Ireland during winter is a warm coat or jacket. It's important to bring one that is both waterproof and lightweight so you can keep warm.

Additionally, you should pack a pair of gloves and a hat to protect your head from the cold wind. You should also bring a scarf to keep your neck warm.

It's also a good idea to pack some comfortable shoes that will allow you to get around easily and comfortably. You can also consider packing some warm socks so you don't get cold feet.

While it is possible to travel to Ireland during the winter, it's a lot easier and safer to travel during the spring or summer. This is because you'll avoid the busiest times of the year, as well as the rainy season and the colder temperatures.

Avoid the Crowds

During the peak of summer, Ireland is a hive of activity and it's hard to escape the throngs of tourists. If you want to see the best of what Ireland has to offer, it is a good idea to plan your itinerary around fewer visitors. Using the right travel planner and a bit of savvy, you should be able to avoid the typical tourist traps and hit the highlights like a pro.

The best way to do this is to book your vacation in advance, and use the internet to find out what's on offer at the time of year you are planning on visiting. There is a wide range of packages available, so you should be able to find something that suits your budget and tastes.

Mistakes to avoid and save time and money while traveling in Ireland

There are some common mistakes that most tourists make when traveling to Ireland. However, if you avoid them, you can save time and money on your trip to Ireland!

The first thing you should do is plan your itinerary ahead of time. This will ensure that you are not spending unnecessary money and will give you the opportunity to see as much of Ireland as possible.

1. Not Planning

When traveling, it is always important to plan ahead. This will help you save time and money while visiting Ireland. If you don't plan your trip correctly, there is a good chance that you will not see all of the attractions on your list or you may not be able to visit them at all.

For example, if you're planning to see the Cliffs of Moher, you should be sure to book your accommodation in advance so you can get the best rate. This will also ensure you have a comfortable and safe experience while on your trip.

Keeping to a strict schedule will also help you stay on budget. If you're trying to see a lot of attractions in a short amount of time, you should consider taking a group tour or creating your own itinerary to maximize your trip. This will save you time and money while avoiding having to purchase new clothes or buying items that aren't needed during your trip.

2. Not Taking Advantage of Discounts

Ireland is a beautiful place and can be an amazing adventure, but it can also cost a lot of money. If you're traveling on a budget, there are some mistakes to avoid so that you can save time and money while traveling in Ireland.

Taking advantage of these discounts will allow you to save money and spend more on the things that are really important to you while you're visiting Ireland. For example, you can save up to 20% on most items in shops and restaurants with a student card.

This is when the country's attractions are most popular and accommodations and car rentals are the most expensive. If you can't avoid traveling in the summer, try to book your vacation during spring or autumn instead. These seasons are much less expensive and the weather is typically a lot better than in the summer.

It's also a good idea to bring some money with you so that you can get cash when you need it.

3. Not Using Public Transport

Ireland is a small country with a compact size that makes it easy to visit many of the major tourist attractions on foot. However, you can also hire a car to explore the island at your own pace and take in the stunning natural scenery on the way.

If you're traveling on a budget, you should consider using public transport as an alternative to renting a car or hiring a tour guide.

You can purchase a Leap Card, which replaces paper tickets and allows you to travel on the rail network and buses in the capital cities of Dublin, Cork and Galway at a hefty discount. You can save over twenty percent on your journey by purchasing one of these cards.

When you're driving in Ireland, make sure to keep in mind that vehicles drive on the left side of the road. This is not only a legal requirement but it's also a good habit to get into while in the country.

Moreover, Irish drivers are very considerate of others on the roads and will nod and give a raised hand or finger as you pass them. This is especially the case on rural country roads where there's often a lot of traffic.

Lastly, be careful not to get a little carried away with the uncanny ability of Irish people to stretch the truth. For example, if an Irish person says 'yeah, it's only down the road', this can mean anywhere from five minutes to 45 minutes.

4. Not Using Leap Cards

When traveling in Ireland, it is important to make use of the TFI Leap Card which provides a convenient and cheap way to pay your fare on busses, trains and DARTs. This smartcard is a contactless payment card that works on Luas trams, buses and DARTs around Dublin, Cork, Galway, Limerick and Waterford city services.

To use your Leap Card, simply touch on and touch off at a validator (on bus, Luas or DART) for each journey. You can also top up your card at Luas or DART ticket machines, convenience stores offering Payzone services and via the iPhone/Android App.

You can also get travel credit for your Leap Card on the Leap website or at a Payzone outlet, which is useful if you plan to visit more than one city during your stay in Ireland. However, there are a few limitations to this method of paying for your travel in Ireland; namely that you must have a credit card with Chip and Pin to load the travel credit onto your Leap Card, and that the credit can only be used in conjunction with an adult or child Leap Card.

The Leap Card is a convenient and affordable way to travel in Ireland, especially for those visiting the country for the first time. It is a great alternative to buying paper tickets for each trip, and it can save you up to 31% on your fares.

Another reason to consider using a Leap Card while traveling in Ireland is that it will allow you to take advantage of other smart discounts like fare capping and the TFI 90 minute Fare in Dublin.

5. Not Taking Advantage of Discounts

The Emerald Isle is a fantastic destination for both first-time and experienced travelers alike. Whether you're looking to experience the rugged natural beauty of the Irish countryside or to soak up all the vibrant culture and history of the country's cities, Ireland has something for everyone.

One of the most common mistakes that tourists make when they visit Ireland is to not take advantage of discounts offered by hotels and other businesses. These discounts can save you a lot of money, especially if you're planning on staying in Ireland for a few days.

Another great way to get discounts when visiting Ireland is to look for group deals. If you're traveling in a large group, most hotels and other businesses will offer discounts on accommodations, flights, and even some meals and activities.

Finally, do not forget to ask about discounts in restaurants. This can save you a huge amount of money and will help ensure that you enjoy the best possible experiences while in Ireland.

There are plenty of things to do and see while you're in Ireland, but it's important to remember that your money is the most valuable asset you have when you're on vacation. You don't want to waste it on a bar or restaurant that isn't worth the price.

Chapter 3.
The Ireland's top attractions

Ireland is an enchanting place to visit and there are so many fantastic attractions to see here. From castles to ancient monuments and even a giant passage tomb, here are some of the top tourist attractions in Ireland!

The ancient and storied Trinity College, in the center of Dublin, is one of Ireland's most revered treasures. This ancient and scholarly institution is truly a world within a world.

Dublin City

Dublin is the capital city of Ireland and is known for its lively atmosphere, historic buildings, and cultural attractions. Visitors can explore the historic Trinity College, which houses the famous Book of Kells, or take a stroll through the picturesque St. Stephen's Green park.

Coastal Ring of Kerry

The Ring of Kerry is a scenic drive that takes visitors through some of Ireland's most stunning landscapes, including rugged coastlines, rolling hills, and picturesque villages. Along the way, visitors can stop at historic sites such as Muckross House and Gardens, or enjoy outdoor activities such as hiking, cycling, and fishing.

Connemara region

The Connemara region of Ireland is a beautiful and rugged area located on the west coast of the country, between the cities of Galway and Westport.

- Kylemore Abbey: Kylemore Abbey is a beautiful 19th-century castle and estate located on the shores of Lough Pollacappul. The abbey is also home to a renowned girls' boarding school.
- Connemara National Park: Connemara National Park covers over 2,000 hectares of rugged wilderness and is home to a variety of wildlife, including red deer, wild goats, and birds of prey.
- Killary Fjord: Killary Fjord is Ireland's only fjord and is a stunning natural attraction located between the Maumturk and Mweelrea Mountains. Visitors can take a boat tour of the fjord to see its dramatic landscapes and spot seals and dolphins, or hike the nearby hills for breathtaking views.
- These are just a few of the top attractions in the Connemara region of Ireland, and visitors can also enjoy outdoor activities such as fishing, kayaking, and horseback riding, or explore the area's traditional Irish culture through language, music, and dance.

Blarney stone fortress

Kissing the stone is not for the faint of heart, as it involves hanging upside down over a drop of several stories, but it is a popular tradition for visitors to Ireland.

In addition to the Blarney Stone, visitors can also explore the castle's impressive architecture and history. The castle was originally built in the 15th century, and its battlements and towers offer stunning views of the surrounding countryside.

The castle grounds also feature beautiful gardens, including the Poison Garden, which contains a variety of poisonous plants and herbs. Visitors can also explore the Rock Close, a magical area that features a druidic circle of standing stones, a wishing steps, and a fairy glade.

Blarney Castle and the Blarney Stone have become a symbol of Irish heritage and culture, and their popularity as a tourist attraction continues to draw visitors from around the world. Whether you believe in the legend of the Blarney Stone or simply appreciate the castle's architecture and history, a visit to this iconic landmark is sure to be a memorable experience for any traveler to Ireland.

Giant's Causeway

The columns, which range in height from a few inches to over 12 meters, form a series of hexagonal stepping stones that lead from the cliffs down to the sea. The formation of the columns is the result of a process known as columnar jointing, which occurs when lava cools rapidly and contracts, causing it to crack into polygonal shapes.

According to local legend, the Giant's Causeway was built by the giant Finn McCool, who wanted to cross the sea to Scotland to fight a rival giant. Finn was said to have built the causeway by laying the hexagonal stones in the sea, forming a bridge to Scotland.

In addition to its geological significance, the Giant's Causeway is also home to a variety of flora and fauna, including rare bird species and a variety of coastal plants. Visitors can explore the surrounding cliffs and headlands on hiking trails, or take a guided tour to learn more about the area's natural and cultural history.

Kylemore Castle

Kylemore Castle, also known as Kylemore Abbey, is a stunning 19th-century castle located in County Galway, Ireland. The castle was built in the late 1800s by Mitchell Henry, a wealthy Englishman who fell in love with the Connemara region of Ireland and decided to build a home there for himself and his wife.

The castle is located on the shore of Lough Pollacappul and is surrounded by beautiful gardens and woodlands. Visitors can take a guided tour of the castle's interior, which features impressive architecture and intricate woodwork. The tour also includes a visit to the Neo-Gothic chapel, which was built by Mitchell Henry in memory of his wife.

In addition to the castle, the Kylemore estate is also home to a variety of gardens and woodlands. The Victorian Walled Garden features a range of colorful flowers, fruits, and vegetables, while the Woodland Walk takes visitors through a forest of native Irish trees.

The Kylemore estate is also home to a Benedictine monastery, which was founded in 1920 when the castle was sold to the Benedictine nuns. Visitors can attend daily mass in the monastery's beautiful chapel and learn about the history of the monastery and the lives of the nuns who live there.

The National Museum of Ireland

The museums are free to enter and offer a fascinating insight into Ireland's history and culture. The museum also houses exhibits on Viking Dublin, medieval Ireland, and the ancient civilizations of Egypt and Cyprus.

The National Museum of Ireland - Decorative Arts and History, also located in Dublin, focuses on the decorative arts and history of Ireland, with exhibits on Irish silver, furniture, ceramics, and glassware. The National Museum of Ireland - Natural History, also located in Dublin, is known as the "Dead Zoo" and houses a collection of over two million specimens of animals from around the world, including many extinct species. The museum also features exhibits on Irish flora and fauna, as well as geological specimens from around the country.

Cork City

Located in the south of Ireland, Cork City is the second-largest city in the country and offers a wide range of attractions for visitors to explore.

One of the main attractions of Cork City is its historic city center, which features a range of architectural styles from various periods of the city's history. The city center is home to several historic landmarks, including the 18th-century English Market, the 19th-century St. Fin Barre's Cathedral, and the 14th-century Red Abbey.

Another popular attraction in Cork City is the University College Cork, which is considered one of the most beautiful university campuses in Europe. The university features a range of historic buildings, including the Gothic revival Main Quadrangle and the stone arches of the O'Rahilly Building.

For those interested in exploring the natural beauty of the region, Cork City offers easy access to several nearby attractions, including the stunning coastline of West Cork, the rugged mountains of the Beara Peninsula, and the scenic Ring of Kerry.

Overall, Cork City offers a unique blend of history, culture, and natural beauty that makes it one of the top attractions in Ireland. Whether you're interested in exploring the city's rich history, enjoying its vibrant arts and cultural scene, or simply soaking up the stunning scenery of the surrounding region, Cork City has something for everyone.

St. Patrick's Cathedral

St. Patrick's Cathedral is one of the most iconic and historically significant landmarks in Ireland. Located in Dublin, it is the largest cathedral in the country and has been an important site of worship for more than 800 years.

The cathedral is named after St. Patrick, the patron saint of Ireland, and is said to stand on the site of a well where he baptized converts to Christianity.

One of the most striking features of St. Patrick's Cathedral is its soaring Gothic architecture, with a towering spire reaching over 40 meters in height. The cathedral is also home to a range of intricate carvings, stained glass windows, and beautiful murals.

The cathedral has played an important role in Irish history, hosting a number of significant events, including the coronation of kings and the marriage of the famous writer Jonathan Swift. The cathedral also features several memorials and monuments to notable figures in Irish history, including William Rowan Hamilton and Arthur Guinness.

Visitors to St. Patrick's Cathedral can explore the historic building and its grounds through guided tours or self-guided visits. The cathedral also hosts regular worship services, concerts, and cultural events throughout the year.

Overall, St. Patrick's Cathedral is a must-visit attraction in Ireland for anyone interested in the country's rich history and culture. Its stunning architecture, historic significance, and beautiful surroundings make it a truly unforgettable experience.

Killarney National Park

One of the main attractions of Killarney National Park is its breathtaking landscapes, which include rolling hills, pristine lakes, and lush forests. The park is home to several of Ireland's highest peaks, including Carrauntoohil, as well as the famous Lakes of Killarney, which are surrounded by stunning mountain scenery.

The Guinness Storehouse

The Guinness Storehouse is a tourist attraction in Dublin, Ireland that takes visitors through the history of the world-famous stout beer. Across seven floors, it tells the story of the brewing process and how Guinness came to be a staple drink worldwide.

The first floor starts with a large atrium that is shaped like a pint glass and is designed to take you back in time. It's a great way to start and will really immerse you in the history of Guinness.

As you move up the atrium you will start to learn about the different parts of the brewing process. Each part is accompanied by dramatic visuals and a wealth of information.

You will also learn how Arthur Guinness took over the brewery in 1759 and grew it into a huge business. As you climb the atrium you will see many of his famous advertising campaigns, which helped to make Guinness such a popular brand.

Once you've finished the tour, it's time to relax and enjoy a glass of your favourite stout at the Gravity Bar on the top floor of the storehouse.

You will get to taste a pint of Guinness while you're here and even pour your own if you purchase the Perfect Pint option. This is a great option if you're a bit of a beer connoisseur and want to try something new!

The Cliffs of Moher

The Cliffs of Moher are one of the most famous landmarks in Ireland and a must-visit during any trip to this island. From sad-eyed puffins to elegantly dressed razorbills, you'll want to take some time to admire the avian life in the area.

The Atlantic Ocean is far below, roaring and crashing against the rocky cliffs. The waves tear at the cliffs, sending out a distinctive sound wave and throwing salt spray high into the air. The most popular place to do this is Doolin, but the Cliffs of Moher are also easily accessible from Liscannor.

If you do want to pay for a tour to the cliffs, there are a few options available to choose from. You can also opt for a self-guided walk which will allow you to explore the cliffs at your own pace.

Another great way to see the cliffs is by walking around Hag's Head. This is a small area with a ruined tower that legend tells us was used as a watch fort for the Cu Chulainn.

The cliffs are a UNESCO Global Geopark and support sustainable tourism. They're a designated refuge for a variety of birds, and are a great place to see enormous numbers of Atlantic puffins nesting in the spring.

Glendalough

If you're looking for a day trip from Dublin, then Glendalough is the place to go. The monastic site is a must-see for history buffs, while the surrounding mountains and lakes make it popular for hikers and outdoor enthusiasts.

Located in the Wicklow Mountains near the town of Roundwood, Glendalough is easy to reach by car or bus. Whether you want to spend one or more days here, you'll be able to see everything that the region has to offer, including waterfalls and rock formations.

A great way to spend a day in Glendalough is to visit the ruins of the monastic city and then take a walk around the Upper or Lower Lake. This makes for a relaxing and peaceful break from the hustle and bustle of the capital.

The monastic settlement was founded in the 6th century by Saint Kevin and features a 30m round tower, a church and a graveyard. Roam the grounds and visit the visitor centre to learn more about the area's rich history.

It's a good idea to get an early start when visiting Glendalough as it tends to get busy later in the day. The most popular place to visit is the Monastic City, but you can also venture a little further out and discover some of the more remote trails.

Another option is to walk along the Miners Walk, a linear trail that winds through the valley of Glendalough's former lead mines. This is the most picturesque way to explore the area, and you'll be able to see the remnants of the mine that operated from 1825 to 1957.

If you're a foodie, then don't miss the restaurant at the Glendalough Hotel. It serves local and international cuisine created with fresh ingredients.

Chapter 4. The "hidden gems" of Ireland

While Ireland has plenty of famous places to visit, there are also many hidden gems that are rarely seen by tourists. From haunted castles to secret caves, here are some of the best off-the-beaten-path sights in Ireland.

Connemara National Park is one of the country's most scenic spots, teeming with wildlife. It's home to the world-famous Twelve Bens, a collection of mountains that give the area its unique character.

Dingle

Dingle is a charming town on Ireland's west coast, surrounded by dramatic landscapes and a fantastic pub scene. A popular jump-off point for touring the Wild Atlantic Way, Dingle Peninsula, and Ring of Kerry, it's a great place to spend a few days.

As well as being one of Ireland's most picturesque fishing towns, Dingle is home to some of the country's best hotels. They have everything from luxury to budget offerings, and all boast awe-inspiring views.

Whether you're in the mood for a spirited drink or you're more into exploring ancient sites, there are plenty of things to do in Dingle. Start your day with a drive along the mighty Slea Head Drive (the most famous part of the peninsula).

If you're into history, don't miss Gallarus Oratory, which is one of the oldest ruins in Ireland. Built around the 6th century, it's a UNESCO World Heritage Site and one of the most impressive sights on the Dingle Peninsula.

You can even get a sneak peak at the local dolphin, Fungie, who has become a main draw for tourists. However, he's still wild and it's important to keep him on his own – don't try to pet him or feed him!

If you're a fan of crystal, don't miss visiting the Dingle Crystal Workshop, where you can watch a master craftsman work on crystal pieces. The owner, Sean Daly, is a Waterford Crystal craftsman who's relocated to Dingle in order to continue his passion for bespoke crystal.

Inch

Located in Lough Swilly, on the south-west coast of Inishowen in County Donegal, Inch is an island in Ireland. It is about 5 square miles (13 km2) in size and has some of the most fertile soil in Donegal.

Inch is one of Ireland's most famous blue flag beaches, but you can also explore its beautiful landscape in a range of other ways. It's a great destination for surfing and other water sports and has surf schools and wetsuit hire available on the beach.

To help document the history of Inch, Donegal County Museums have collaborated with a team of experts from Norway, Iceland, and Northern Ireland on an international heritage project, CINE, which is focused on capturing the rich and fascinating life of the island using aerial photography, video, and 3D mapping. The CINE project aims to create an interactive, virtual museum that will inspire and educate visitors about the island's unique history and cultural heritage.

At the beginning of the 20th century a number of large and small drains were constructed to divert a section of the tidal waters of Lough Swilly away from the island. This drained much of the mud flats, which would have caused serious problems if left flooded.

Over the years, the slobs have become steadily less salty and the drains have been improved to a good standard. However, the tidal extremes and other factors have a continued effect on the health of the island.

At the extreme seaward end of Inch Island, the ruins of Inch Castle stand as a reminder of what it was like to live and work on this island in the past. Built in the mid 15th century, it was a valuable viewpoint and defence point for the island, protecting Cahir O'Doherty's heartlands. It was later granted to Arthur Chichester, Lord Deputy of Ireland.

Kinsale

Located along the Wild Atlantic Way, Kinsale is one of Ireland's most picturesque and historical towns. It is a popular tourist destination, renowned for its scenic harbor and delicious food.

When you visit Kinsale, you can't miss the town center, which is surrounded by brightly-coloured shops and restaurants that will leave you wanting to stay for longer. You can also take a walk to the Old Head of Kinsale, which is an excellent hike that will make you feel like you're in the midst of nature.

For a more understated, yet fun hidden gem in Kinsale, you should visit the Poet's Corner Cafe! This mid-range priced cafe serves up delicious breakfasts, sandwiches and coffees. What's more, they have a unique book exchange that allows you to bring in your own books and trade them for others!

You can even book an impromptu tour with them if you're looking to learn more about the local culture and taste some of the best food in Kinsale!

Kinsale is a small town that doesn't offer Michelin-recommended restaurants, but it does have plenty of cafes and pubs that serve up mouthwatering dishes. Kinsale is also known as the 'Gourmet Capital of Ireland,' so it's worth stopping by any of these places to get a bite to eat!

Murphy's Ice Cream Parlour

If you're looking for a hefty scoop of ice cream in the capital of Ireland, look no further than Murphy's. Their ice-free scoops are the stuff of dreams and they're the best of their kind in the city. Their slick service and tasty elixirs are a must if you're in the mood to shop around. The company has a solid customer base, largely thanks to its slick new digs and stellar menu. The company is a true family business with a well rounded team of employees who can be counted on for a friendly and informative experience. The best part is that you can try a bit of everything without having to leave the building!

Kerry International Dark-Sky Reserve

The night sky has always fascinated people in Ireland, and it's no surprise that the country has a few stargazing sites of its own. Many Neolithic monuments in the Iveragh Peninsula were built to align with the sun and stars, including a Bronze Age stone circle at Bonane Heritage Park near Kenmare.

Several other spots in the region are designated as dark-sky reserves, and if you're lucky enough to visit one of these places, you can enjoy spectacular views of the Milky Way and faint meteors with no need for special equipment. The area is protected from light pollution by the Kerry Mountains and Atlantic Ocean, making it a prime spot for stargazing.

It's also a great place to observe the phases of the moon and astronomical events, such as aurora displays. To see these sights, you need clear skies and an unobstructed view of the Milky Way.

While the best time to see the night sky in Kerry is during the summer solstice, you can experience it year-round. In fact, the IDA lists this as one of the top European destinations for stargazing during the winter solstice.

To get the most out of your stargazing adventure, it's important to plan ahead. To be sure you don't miss the most spectacular show, check out this guide to the best times of year to visit the Kerry International Dark-Sky Reserve.

To be eligible for IDA certification as an International Dark Sky Reserve, an applicant must complete the rigorous application process and document category-specific program requirements. You can learn more about the process here.

Chapter 5.
The local culture of Ireland

Too often people travel to a new country without truly getting in touch with the local culture. They may visit a few landmarks, snap a few photos and eat at a few restaurants, but what about the deeper side of things?

1. Eat the local cuisine

Whether you're traveling for business or pleasure, eating the local cuisine can help you get in touch with the local culture. The dishes of a certain region reflect its history and traditions, and the foods of a particular country can tell you a lot about that place's resources, climate, and environment. For example, the food of coastal regions usually features seafood, while the cuisine of mountainous countries often focuses on hearty meat dishes.

2. Go off the beaten path

Traveling off the beaten path can be a fantastic way to get in touch with the local culture and experience a place from a different perspective. This can be done through a variety of ways, from eating the local cuisine to taking part in cultural exchange activities.

If you're planning to go off the beaten path, one of the best ways to make sure that you experience it safely is to plan your trip carefully. This includes conducting thorough research, connecting with locals, and choosing accommodations and activities that prioritize safety.

Going off the beaten path can also lead to discovering lesser-known historical sites, monuments, and museums that offer a deeper understanding of the past. These hidden gems often reveal interesting stories and offer a more tranquil and intimate atmosphere than their more famous counterparts.

3. Learn a few words in the local language

A trip to a foreign country will be far more enjoyable when you know some words in the local language. This will make navigating restaurants, markets and even train stations a breeze!

It will also show the locals that you are taking a genuine interest in their culture and are not afraid to put in the effort to learn a little.

One of the best ways to start learning a few words in the local language is by using apps like Duolingo or Babbel. However, if you're looking to really immerse yourself in the local culture and language, you should practice with a real-life native instead of relying on your phone.

4. Talk to the locals

Talking to the locals is an essential part of any traveler's journey. It helps you build your confidence and feel more connected to a country.

Make a point of talking to your hotel staff, tour guides, taxi drivers, waiters and grocery store clerks. They will all want to help you learn about their country and share their knowledge.

5. Take the local transport

One of the best ways to experience a new destination is to hop on the local transport and let the locals guide you. Not only will you be able to get around for cheap, but you'll also be rewarded with the opportunity to see your destination from a different vantage point.

Taking the train is an excellent way to get in touch with a new country's culture, while bus travel allows you to mingle with the locals.

You might be surprised at just how many people don't take advantage of these options. Taking the local transport also helps you learn the intricacies of the local language and get a true feel for your destination.

6. Stay in a local home

When staying in a local home, you get the best chance to truly immerse yourself in the local culture. This is especially important if you choose to join a home exchange agency that allows you to live in a different host's apartment or house for a period of time.

Another way to immerse yourself in the local culture is by eating at restaurants and shopping at stores that are frequented by the locals. You may even be surprised to find that you can eat and shop in areas that are not crowded with tourists! It's also a good idea to take the bus or tram rather than relying on taxis, as this is a great way to see more of the city and connect with local people. Plus, this will save you a lot of money!

7. Go to local events

Whether you are going on vacation or living abroad, finding events and activities in your destination is a great way to connect with the local culture. From concerts to sports events, holiday festivities to art walks, there are so many opportunities to experience something new and exciting in a new country.

Facebook is one of the best sources for locating local events. They have an event search that will detect your location and recommend local events that line up with what you're looking for.

Ticketmaster is another excellent resource for attending live music, theater and sporting events. Their app allows you to see all the event details, find the seat location and check the price. You can also purchase tickets directly from the app.

8. Take part in local festivals

Festivals are a great way to get in touch with the local culture. They can be organised by local councils and offer a range of events and attractions to take part in.

Communities can also hold festivals of their own. They can be held for a number of reasons, including religion, art, music, and harvest time.

Festivals are a good way of promoting community pride, which can help residents to feel more connected to their local area and contribute positively to its development. Moreover, they can also boost tourism.

9. Visit a local museum

Museums are a great way to get in touch with the local culture. They offer visual arts and audio guides that give you an insight into the history and heritage of a country or city.

They also play a vital role in cultural preservation by documenting artifacts and preserving them. This ensures that local culture is preserved and can be passed down from generation to generation.

To avoid the crowds, Nick Gray, founder of museum tour company Museum Hack, recommends visiting during a late-night opening. This will allow you to enter the museum without having to stand in a long queue and will give you a chance to see the exhibits that interest you most.

Besides being a great way to learn about a place's history and culture, museums have become hot-spots for community engagement.

Tips for avoiding crowds

Whether you're planning a trip to Ireland for the first time or you've been there before, you'll want to make sure that you get the most out of your vacation.

1. Book your accommodation in advance

One of the most important tips while traveling in Ireland is to book your accommodation in advance. This is especially important if you are planning to visit Ireland during the busy summer season, as hotel prices tend to skyrocket in these times.

Alternatively, consider visiting Ireland during the shoulder seasons (April, May, June, September or October) when hotels are less expensive and attractions are a little less crowded. This time of year also allows travelers to take advantage of some last-minute deals.

The main reason to book your accommodation in advance is because it can help you save a lot of money. Moreover, it can also ensure that you don't have to worry about your accommodation being booked by other travelers.

For example, many hotels and hostels offer free or discounted pick-ups from the airport/train station or bus terminal when you make a reservation. However, it is important to read the small print of these offers before you decide to take advantage of them.

Another good way to book your accommodation in advance is to use a travel agent. Most travel agents will have access to a large database of hotels and hostels in your destination. They can then contact them on your behalf and make reservations for you.

If you are looking for a budget-friendly option, you might want to look into B&Bs. These types of lodgings are often much cheaper than hotels and offer a more authentic Irish experience.

If you are traveling alone, you might also want to consider booking your first and last nights in the same hotel or hostel so that you don't have to stress about making arrangements on the fly. This can save you a lot of time and stress while you are in the country.

2. Plan your itinerary in advance

Planning in advance can help you get the most out of your trip. You can do things like read books, maps, destination guides, and cookbooks about the place you're visiting. This will not only help you familiarize yourself with the area, but also make it easier to decide what to do when you're there.

Another way to plan in advance is by making a list of things you want to see and do during your trip. This will help you avoid being lost and overwhelmed when you arrive in Ireland.

Besides, it will help you create an itinerary that fits your specific needs and interests. This will allow you to maximize your time and see all the highlights of the country without exhausting yourself!

To make your itinerary as smooth as possible, plan it out at least a month in advance. This gives you enough time to book restaurants, museums and special entries that may require a specific date.

You can even book your transportation for the trip if you prefer to do so. This will help you save money and ensure you don't have to worry about getting around when you arrive in Ireland.

When it comes to the weather, you're likely to encounter some rain during your trip. This is why it's important to pack an umbrella or a raincoat for every day of your stay!

If you're a solo traveler, it is highly recommended that you book your flight and accommodation in advance. This will ensure that you have the best available options and prices for your trip. Additionally, you will have more flexibility to change or cancel your bookings if something is not working out for you.

3. Take your time to explore

One of the best ways to experience a new country is to explore its countryside and rural towns. These areas are full of history, culture, and natural beauty. Unlike major cities, these towns don't have all the crowds and tourist attractions, so you can enjoy a more authentic and meaningful Irish experience.

If you're looking for an immersive and educational way to discover the real Ireland, book a guided tour. These will give you a knowledgeable guide who will show you the best parts of the country while keeping you safe and avoiding scams.

Another good option is to rent a car and go on a road trip around the island. This will give you the chance to drive through the scenic roads and visit unique sights like the Dark Hedges in Northern Ireland.

The Cliffs of Moher are an iconic sight in Ireland, but the country is also home to some of the most impressive monuments in Europe. For example, Newgrange is a prehistoric monument that is older than Stonehenge and the Egyptian pyramids.

Finally, don't miss out on a visit to the famous Quiet Man Bridge. This is one of the best-known bridges in Ireland and has appeared in numerous movies.

It is also important to know that Irish people are very friendly and will be happy to help you out when possible. This is especially true in rural areas and smaller towns where you'll be able to connect with locals.

4. Get a local SIM card

While traveling to a new country, it is very important to have access to a local SIM card. This will ensure that you will be able to make and receive calls, text messages, and use data while traveling.

One of the main reasons why you should consider getting a local SIM card while traveling in Ireland is that it will save you money. Unlike international roaming, which will charge you by the day for your data usage, you can use a local SIM to avoid high per-minute charges and other costs associated with using a foreign carrier's network.

Another good reason to consider getting a local SIM while traveling in Ireland is that it will work in multiple countries across the European Union. This is a huge advantage for those who are planning to visit many different European countries on their trip.

Buying a local SIM while traveling in Ireland is easy, but there are a few things that you need to keep in mind. The first thing is to check whether your phone is compatible with the frequencies used in Ireland. If it is, then you will be able to use it without any issues. This will allow you to enjoy a better travel experience.

5. Don't be afraid to tip

Tipping isn't required while traveling in Ireland, but it can be a nice gesture. Leaving a tip is a great way to show your gratitude for the good service you've received.

When dining out, it's common to tip waiters 10-15% of the total bill. Some restaurants will add a service charge to your bill, which is why you should leave more than the usual amount.

If you're satisfied with the service you receive, you should also tip your hotel porter and housekeeping staff. You can tip them EUR1 - EUR2 per bag brought to your room, and around EUR5 for their services.

At bars, you may be asked to tip the bartender. This is a normal practice in many countries, and it's a small gesture.

Irish pubs are popular spots for travelers to meet and drink, but be sure to tip the bartender if you're happy with the service. You can leave a EUR1 to EUR2 tip for table service, or simply offer to treat the bartender to something later on in the night.

Another thing to keep in mind when traveling in Ireland is that there are petty crimes, such as theft, burglary and purse snatching, especially in tourist areas. It's a good idea to carry a fanny pack or security wallet in crowded areas, as well as lock your rental car and use an alarm system if possible.

You can also learn some important Irish slang while traveling in Ireland, which will help you communicate more easily. For example, it's common to use the phrase "F-word" in daily conversation in Ireland. This is not a swear word, but it's a term that Irish people use for disagreement or to express their feelings.

Ireland's best restaurants, clubs and nightlife

With an exciting social scene and a diverse range of bars and restaurants, Limerick is a vibrant and fun city.

It has a great selection of bars for both traditional Irish live music and quiet pints. Whether you are looking for something to do with a group of friends or a romantic spot for a date, you'll be sure to find what you need in Limerick.

Blakes of the Hollow

Renowned for its pints of stout and Irish coffees, Blakes of the Hollow is one of County Fermanagh's oldest pubs. It has been recommended by Georgina Campbell's

Jameson Guide and is also a must-visit for anyone wanting to experience the best of Enniskillen.

It is a classic Victorian bar and is known for its snugs, which are popular with people of all ages. It has a huge range of drinks and is a great place to meet up with friends.

Joe Blake, who owns the pub with his brother Mark, says that a lot of people visit the bar for its history. He said: "My father bought it in 1929 and he was very proud of it, but he always refused to have it modernised. He always said he wanted it to be a traditional pub and that's what it is.

The pub has a number of regulars including Colm Toibin who described it as a 'cathedral of a pub' and the late John McGahern. He was a big fan of Blakes and would often travel up to collect his letters from the bar.

Another great thing about Blakes is that it is a very popular spot for music. It has traditional music sessions every Friday night and is a must-visit for anyone wanting a real taste of Ireland.

The pub has a number of famous guests who frequent it, including Rory McIlroy's parents and Charlie Lawson who was the man responsible for a photograph of the cast of Coronation Street. It is a popular spot for tourists and locals alike. It has a huge range of different beers and is a great place to enjoy live music and a good drink.

JJ Houghs

JJ Houghs is a pub that has been generating a lot of buzz recently. Located in Banagher, this 250-year-old establishment is known for its charm and warm welcome. It also makes a great stop off point for boaters who are taking river cruises in the nearby majestic River Shannon.

It has been named one of the best bars in Ireland by Lonely Planet, and is an Irish institution for good reason. Its dazzling array of cocktails, booze-centric beverage program, and old-school wood paneled interior make it an excellent destination for both locals and tourists alike.

Besides its stellar drinks program and snazzy design, the sandstone and timber-clad pub boasts a wealth of character thanks to its traditional shopfront, decorative console brackets, and a few clever gimmicks like an octagonal bar top. For those who are in the mood for something a little more sophisticated, this pub also offers a range of wine and beer.

The most impressive feature of this establishment is its swanky cocktail menu, which features a number of unique concoctions such as their Dutch Gold. It is also a great spot for a light bite, with its pizza-centric menu.

In addition to being a fantastic night out, the venue is also dog-friendly with indoor and outdoor seating available. The bar even provides water bowls for your furry friends!

The swanky glass-enclosed bar is the brainchild of owner Ger Hough. It was one of his visions in reimagining the local landmark to create a space that celebrates the area's best and brightest. The result is a place where locals can nab some of the most memorable tipples in town while enjoying a wholesome meal and a few laughs.

Kelly's Complex

The Kelly's complex in Portrush is home to the Bistro, The Deerstalker Bar, Kon Tiki Boat Bar and Kelly's Village. Featuring the best restaurants and nightlife Northern Ireland has to offer, it has become a popular hangout for locals and visitors.

A visit to this iconic venue is a must on every visitor's bucket list. It's the perfect place to enjoy great food, drink a cold beer and listen to live music. Located just off the main road, Kelly's complex is the perfect spot to soak up the sun on a warm summer's day or enjoy a night out with friends.

What sets Kelly's apart from the rest is their selection of craft beers, cocktails and a menu with something for everyone. Their chefs are also known for their dedication to quality and their commitment to making sure every guest has a great experience.

It's not often that you find a place that has a well thought out drink specials and food menu as well as a world class jukebox, so if you are a fan of Irish pub grub, Kelly's is the perfect place to visit. For more information on their drink specials and menu check out their website or contact them on Facebook. You can also take a tour of their facilities by booking an in-house tour! The tours are a great way to see the hidden gems of this thriving venue.

Lowry's Bar

Located in Clifden, Ireland, Lowry's Bar is one of the best restaurants clubs and nightlife in Connemara. The pub serves a variety of traditional Irish music, along with over 115 whiskeys and creamy pints of Guinness.

In addition to being a great place for a pint of Guinness, it is also renowned for its wholesome bar food. The food is simple and delicious, making it a popular choice among locals and tourists alike.

The bar is known for its friendly and welcoming staff, so it is always a good idea to stop by for a chat and some great food. You can even enjoy live music during the evening.

Another top spot for a great night out is Lahinch, a beach town that is known for its social scene and waves. Its youth-heavy population draws in wave chasers and beach babies year-round, making it a fun and dynamic place to hang out.

There is a plethora of bars in Lahinch, so there is always something to keep you entertained. Some of the best bars in Lahinch are Flanagans, O'Looney's, and The Nineteenth Bar.

Founded in 1949 by Patrick Lowry, who was stationed in Donegal for a short period of time, the establishment soon became well-known for its unique selling point: it was not only a public house but also a grocery. This was extremely useful for people who were going shopping or needed to pick up a few items that they didn't need at home.

The establishment also has a number of classic arcade games for people to play. The bar also offers private couch seating if you're looking to get away from the crowds and relax with a cold one.

Temple Bar

The Temple Bar district is home to some of Ireland's best restaurants clubs and nightlife. Located between O'Connell Street and the South Georgian district, it's a vibrant area that's popular with tourists and locals alike.

While the neighborhood was once famed for sexy brothels and urban decay, today it's home to a range of high-end hotels, restaurants, and cafes. It also contains a number of creative destinations including art galleries and design shops.

Whether you're looking for a dram of whiskey, an authentic Irish dish, some live music or just a chance to get to know the locals, you'll find everything you need at one of these top pubs in Temple Bar. Regardless of where you decide to go, it's guaranteed that you'll have a great time!

If you're looking for a lively music session in Dublin, you can't go wrong with The Auld Dubliner. It's a buzzy place where you could spend an entire night listening to live sessions from a wide variety of artists.

For a slightly more swanky experience, Vintage Cocktail Club is a hidden gem in Temple Bar. This 1920s-style clandestine bar serves up an extensive list of spirits and specially crafted cocktails. It's perfect for that secret rendezvous, a pre-show cocktail or a late night party!

With a long list of classic cocktails and modern twists, The Porterhouse in Parliament St is another place that's worth checking out. It's an ultra-popular bar that weighs out equal in tourists to locals and is sure to be hopping any night of the week!

While it might not be the most sophisticated pub in Temple Bar, it's a great choice for a quick drink before heading out. The menu includes traditional Irish dishes, and it's also a good choice for vegetarians or those with special dietary requirements.

List of typical Irish foods and drinks to try on a trip to Ireland

A typical Irish breakfast is an all-you-can-eat fry-up that includes bacon, sausages, eggs, tomatoes and hash browns along with black and white pudding (pork meat with oatmeal and blood sausage). It can also include toast and tea to keep you going for a whole day of sightseeing.

1. Guinness

A trip to Ireland isn't complete without trying some of the country's most famous and traditional foods and drinks.

Typical Irish food is simple, hearty dishes that follow age-old family recipes.

Drinks to try on a trip to Ireland include Guinness, which is the country's national drink. While it isn't always easy to find a proper Irish pub that serves only Guinness, the drink does travel well. It's one of the reasons that it's become so popular in other countries, too.

Its popularity in American cities with large Irish populations has also contributed to its widespread appeal. But Guinness is actually quite different in America than it is in Ireland.

In America, draft lines are regulated by a three-tier system that leaves it up to bars and restaurants to maintain and care for their brews. In Ireland, however, the company is directly involved with draft lines, ensuring that they are properly maintained and functioning correctly. While this doesn't necessarily mean that a pint of Guinness tastes better in the Irish countryside, it does have a stronger local flavor. You'll have to make a trip to Ireland to experience this for yourself, but it's certainly worth the effort.

2. Irish Whiskey

As you might know, Ireland is a popular tourist destination for its stunning scenery and rich history. Its thriving culinary scene is also one of its main draws. You can easily find Michelin-starred restaurants or cozy pubs serving traditional Irish dishes.

The country is also home to some of the world's best whiskey distilleries. You can visit them if you want to get a taste of the process behind their products.

Irish Whiskey is usually distilled using unmalted barley that is triple-distilled. This results in a smooth and sweet flavour profile.

It is also distilled differently than Scotch Whisky. First, the place of production is important: Scotch can only be made in Scotland, while Irish Whiskey may be made anywhere in Ireland, including the Republic and Northern Ireland.

Second, the method of production is important: in Scotland, spirits are distilled twice, but Irish whiskeys are often distilled three times in pot stills. This process removes unpleasant sulfur compounds that can make them taste very bad.

Third, the age of the whiskey is important: older whiskeys have a better flavor and a higher alcohol content. The Irish tradition of maturing whiskey in oak casks allows them to retain a more complex and subtle flavor.

If you want to try some Irish whiskey, it's important to pick a good quality one that you like. You can find many brands and styles of whiskey in the market, so you should choose a bottle that suits your tastes.

3. Seaweed

Seaweed is a type of algae that grows in the ocean and in other bodies of water, such as rivers and lakes. It's an important food source for countless marine species and provides many health benefits to humans as well.

In Ireland, there are many ways to use seaweed. You can eat it raw, or you can make it into a delicious drink, such as Seaweed Set Milk (which I enjoyed at the Blue Bar in Dublin).

But the most popular way to eat seaweed is to add it into recipes, such as Seaweed Salad and the Irish Umami (a concentrated mix of kombu seaweed extract and seawater). The umami flavor enhancer has been a favorite ingredient for Irish chefs for years, and can be added to soups, salads, and desserts as an extra boost of flavor.

In addition to adding flavor, seaweed is also an excellent source of nutrients, including calcium, copper, iodine, and iron. It is also a good source of fiber, which can help reduce your risk of heart disease and cancer.

4. Soda Bread

Soda bread is one of the most common and traditional Irish foods, with recipes passed down through generations of families. It is a simple yet delicious bread that is made with a few ingredients - flour, baking soda, salt and buttermilk. It is a very easy to make and can be served warm or at room temperature.

It is also a perfect choice for breakfast, especially with a bowl of tea. The flavour is mild and you can top it with your favourite jams, marmalade, clotted cream and other toppings. It is a great accompaniment to hearty stews, but it is also suitable for dunking in a creamy Irish butter or dripping over a plate of fresh fruit.

Throughout Ireland, there are different types of soda bread, but all are pretty much the same. They are made with the same basic ingredients and usually come in a round loaf with a cross shape on top.

The only difference is that some people add raisins to the recipe. Others add a mix of nuts, raisins and dried cranberries for a more sweet taste.

Soda bread is a popular recipe in many different countries, including the Americas, Scotland and Ireland. It is a simple and tasty bread that can be enjoyed with a cup of tea. It can be made with a few different ingredients and is perfect to serve for breakfast, lunch or dinner.

5. Kerrygold Butter

Ireland's rich green landscape is home to a plethora of dairy products, including some of the world's finest butter. Kerrygold, a popular brand of butter, has long been one of the country's most widely distributed butters.

The butter is made from the milk of Irish dairy cows. These animals graze on the grass that grows on the Irish hills, producing milk with a bright yellow hue. It also contains a high amount of butterfat, which is essential to creating an incredibly creamy product that's perfect for spreading on scones, toast or cookies.

A favorite among chefs and bakers alike, Kerrygold is available in both salted and unsalted varieties. While unsalted butter is not as common as salted, it's still an excellent choice for anyone trying to control their salt intake.

Founded in 1962, Kerrygold is still a beloved brand of butter and can be found in most grocery stores. Its 82 percent butterfat content makes it perfect for baking and making pastries.

Another typical Irish food that can be found in countless restaurants across the country is chowder, an iconic Irish dish that features seafood with thick broth. It's a great addition to any meal and can be served in a wide range of styles.

While there are many other typical Irish foods and drinks to try on a trip to Ireland, you can't visit the Emerald Isle without taking a taste of the nation's delicious traditional cuisine. Start your trip with a hearty bowl of chowder or a slice of soda bread and then move on to a piping hot plate of black pudding, Irish salmon or a juicy steak.

6. Baked Ham

One of the most common and popular traditional Irish foods is baked ham. It is a great meal for all occasions and can be prepared in a variety of ways. It is easy to prepare and can be served hot or cold. It is a delicious main dish that can feed a large number of people. It can also be used in a variety of other dishes such as sandwiches, soups and frittatas. Oftentimes, a large piece of ham is glazed with a sweet-flavoured glaze to make it even more appetizing. The best way to prepare a baked ham is to ensure that the ham is thoroughly heated before you apply the glaze. This will help it to stay moist and tender. If you are using a bone-in ham, you should allow it to cook until it has reached the right temperature (it will take longer to heat through than a boneless ham). Once it has reached this temperature, you can remove it from the oven and brush on the glaze. Many authors recommend covering the ham with foil to keep it from drying out. The foil should come off in the last thirty minutes of cooking to let the glaze caramelise and thicken. A variety of spices are used to flavour the ham. These include cinnamon, allspice and ginger. A small amount of nutmeg is also used in some recipes. A few recipes also include cloves in the ham to give it an extra bit of flavour.

Chapter 6.
The best places to stay

Ireland is a beautiful country with a rich history and diverse culture, making it a popular travel destination.

- Dublin: If you're looking for a vibrant and lively city experience, Dublin is the place to be.
- Cork: Cork is a vibrant city with a rich culinary scene and plenty of historic landmarks. Some of the best places to stay in Cork include the city center, the historic Shandon neighborhood, and the scenic coastal town of Kinsale.
- Killarney: If you're looking for natural beauty and outdoor activities, Killarney is a great choice. This picturesque town is situated near the Ring of Kerry and boasts stunning scenery and plenty of hiking and biking trails.
- Dingle: Dingle is a quaint and charming coastal town that's perfect for a relaxing getaway. You'll find plenty of cozy bed and breakfasts and

boutique hotels in Dingle, as well as traditional Irish pubs and restaurants.

In terms of accommodation, Ireland has something for everyone, whether you're looking for budget-friendly options or luxurious hotels. Some of the best hotels in Ireland include the Shelbourne Hotel in Dublin, the Ashford Castle in County Mayo, and the Ballyfin Demesne in County Laois. If you're traveling on a budget, consider staying in a hostel or bed and breakfast, which can be found throughout the country.

Ultimately, the best places to stay in Ireland will depend on your interests and travel plans. Whether you're looking for city life, outdoor adventures, or a relaxing seaside getaway, Ireland has it all.

Hotels:

- The Shelbourne Hotel, Dublin - A luxurious five-star hotel located in the heart of Dublin. The Shelbourne is known for its historic elegance and impeccable service.
- The Westbury, Dublin - A stylish and sophisticated hotel located in the heart of Dublin's shopping and entertainment district.
- The Europe Hotel & Resort, Killarney - A five-star hotel located on the shores of Killarney's famous lake. The Europe is known for its stunning scenery and luxurious amenities.
- Ashford Castle, Cong - A five-star castle hotel located in the picturesque village of Cong. Ashford Castle is known for its rich history and luxurious accommodations.
- The Merrion Hotel, Dublin - A luxurious five-star hotel located in the heart of Dublin's Georgian Quarter. The Merrion is known for its art collection and Michelin-starred restaurant.

Airbnb:

- Charming Cottage in the Countryside, Cork - A cozy and rustic cottage located in the heart of Cork's countryside. This Airbnb is perfect for

those looking to escape the hustle and bustle of city life.
- Seaside Retreat, Galway - A charming Airbnb located just steps from the beach in the scenic town of Galway. This Airbnb is perfect for those looking for a relaxing seaside getaway.
- Bright and Spacious Apartment, Dublin - A modern and stylish apartment located in the heart of Dublin's city center. This Airbnb is perfect for those looking to explore the city's vibrant nightlife and cultural attractions.
- Traditional Irish Cottage, County Mayo - A charming and authentic Irish cottage located in the scenic countryside of County Mayo. This Airbnb is perfect for those looking for a peaceful and authentic Irish experience.
- Riverside House, Killarney - A spacious and modern house located on the banks of the River Flesk in the scenic town of Killarney. This Airbnb is perfect for those looking to explore the town's natural beauty and outdoor activities.

Chapter 7. Activities

Spending time together strengthens family bonds and creates positive behaviours. This is also a great way to relieve stress and bring people closer together.

It is important to get away from the TV and devices, and reconnect with your family on a regular basis. This list of family bonding activities will provide quality time and build lasting memories.

1. Go on a picnic

Picnics are a great way for families to spend time together and enjoy the beautiful scenery of Ireland. Here are some ideas for activities that you can do as a family during your picnic:

- Explore the area: Take a walk around the area where you have set up your picnic. You can look for wildlife, interesting plants or simply enjoy the scenery.
- Play games: Bring along some outdoor games such as frisbee, soccer ball, or a badminton set. These games can be enjoyed by everyone and are a great way to get active and have fun together.
- Storytelling: Share family stories or read a book out loud to each other. This can be a fun way to bond and learn more about each other.
- Arts and crafts: Bring some paper, colored pencils or paint, and let everyone create their own masterpiece inspired by the beautiful surroundings.
- Enjoy a picnic feast: Bring along some tasty treats such as sandwiches, fruits, and snacks to enjoy together. You can also have a BBQ or cookout if it's allowed in the area.
- Capture memories: Take photos of the beautiful scenery, your family enjoying the picnic, and the activities you do together. These photos will be a great way to remember your special day out.

Remember to pack sunscreen, hats, and plenty of water to stay hydrated during your picnic. And always leave the area clean and tidy when you leave to help preserve the beauty of the environment for future generations.

2. Visit the library

If you're looking for a fun way to spend a few hours with your family, consider visiting the library. It's an underrated resource that can be a great way to learn, socialize and have fun as a family for free!

Visiting the library in Ireland can be a fun and educational activity for people of all ages. Here are some fun activities you can do while visiting the library in Ireland:

- Attend a reading or storytelling event: Many libraries in Ireland offer reading or storytelling events for children and adults. These events can be a fun way to learn and engage with literature, and to connect with the community.
- Explore the library's collection: Libraries in Ireland have a wide variety of books, magazines, newspapers, and other resources available for loan. Take some time to browse the shelves and discover new authors and genres.
- Participate in a book club: Many libraries in Ireland have book clubs that meet regularly to discuss a selected book. This is a great way to connect with other readers, learn more about literature, and engage in thoughtful conversations.
- Attend a workshop or class: Many libraries in Ireland offer workshops and classes on a variety

of topics, including creative writing, computer skills, and language learning. These can be fun and educational activities to participate in.
- Play board games: Some libraries in Ireland have board games available to play. This can be a fun way to pass the time, and to connect with other library visitors.
- Use the library's digital resources: Many libraries in Ireland offer access to digital resources such as e-books, audiobooks, and online databases. Take advantage of these resources to learn something new or enjoy a good book.

Remember to be respectful of other library visitors and to follow the library's rules and guidelines. Libraries are a great resource for education, entertainment, and community engagement, and visiting them can be a fun and rewarding experience.

3. Attend a community concert

Seeing live music is fun for all involved, and attending a free community concert can be a great way to spend a summer night. These events are typically held in local parks, and they can be a fun way to get out of the house and enjoy some quality family time.

When it comes to attending a concert with the whole family, there are many things to consider, from where you're going to sit to whether or not your kids will enjoy it. Some concerts have child-friendly seating options, and others will require a little extra planning to make sure everyone has a great time.

Attending a community concert in Ireland is a great way to immerse yourself in the local culture, enjoy live music, and connect with the community. Here are some fun activities you can do while attending a community concert:

- Sing along to the music: Whether you know the lyrics or not, singing along to the music is a great way to engage with the performance and show your appreciation.
- Dance to the music: If the music is upbeat and lively, get up and dance! This can be a fun way to let loose and enjoy the energy of the music and the crowd.
- Meet new people: Community concerts are a great opportunity to connect with people in the local area. Strike up a conversation with someone sitting next to you, or join a group of people dancing to the music.
- Try local food and drink: Many community concerts in Ireland offer food and drink stalls where you can sample local cuisine and drinks. This can be a fun way to try something new and support local vendors.
- Take photos or videos: Capture memories of the concert by taking photos or videos of the performance, the crowd, and the atmosphere. These photos and videos can be a great way to remember the experience and share it with others.
- Support the artists: Many community concerts in Ireland feature local artists or musicians. Show your support by purchasing their merchandise, following them on social media, or attending their future performances.

Attending a community concert in Ireland is a fun and festive way to connect with the local community, enjoy live music, and create lasting memories. Be sure to check the schedule of local events in advance to find a concert that suits your musical tastes and interests.

4. Visit a beach

One of the best ways to spend a day as a family is by visiting a beach. It's a great way to unwind and recharge, plus you can find activities and things to do that are free in the area.

Visiting the beaches in Ireland can be a fun and relaxing activity, especially during the summer months. Here are some fun activities you can do while visiting the beach:

- Build a sandcastle: Building a sandcastle is a classic beach activity that can be enjoyed by people of all ages. Get creative and build a castle, a moat, or even a whole sand city.
- Swim in the sea: If the water temperature is warm enough, take a swim in the sea. Swimming is a great way to cool off on a hot day and get some exercise.
- Play beach volleyball or soccer: Bring a ball and play a game of beach volleyball or soccer. These games can be enjoyed by groups of people and are a great way to get active and have fun.
- Go for a beach walk: Take a leisurely walk along the beach, enjoying the fresh air and the scenery. This can be a relaxing way to spend time with family or friends.
- Picnic on the beach: Pack a picnic lunch and enjoy it on the beach. This can be a fun way to enjoy the scenery and the company of loved ones.

- Collect seashells: Take a walk along the beach and collect seashells. This can be a fun way to explore the beach and create a keepsake of your visit.

Remember to follow beach safety guidelines and respect the environment by leaving the beach clean and free of litter. The beaches in Ireland are a beautiful and enjoyable destination, and visiting them can be a fun way to spend a day with family or friends.

5. Visit a lighthouse

Lighthouses are iconic structures that have been used for centuries to guide mariners in dangerous ocean waters. They are also a beautiful sight to see and provide spectacular views.

A visit to a lighthouse is a great way to get some quality time with your children, while at the same time learning about history and maritime culture. Most lighthouses are free to visit and many have family-friendly events that will make your visit even more enjoyable!

Visiting a lighthouse in Ireland can be a fun and educational activity for people of all ages. Here are some fun activities you can do while visiting a lighthouse:

- Take a guided tour: Many lighthouses in Ireland offer guided tours that provide insights into the history of the lighthouse, its architecture, and its significance to the local area. This can be a fun and informative way to learn more about the lighthouse and its role in maritime history.
- Climb to the top: Many lighthouses in Ireland allow visitors to climb to the top for stunning views of the surrounding area. This can be a fun and rewarding way to experience the lighthouse and the surrounding landscape.
- Learn about maritime history: Lighthouses have played a vital role in maritime history, and visiting a lighthouse can be a great way to learn about the history of maritime navigation and the important role that lighthouses have played in keeping ships and sailors safe.
- Spot marine wildlife: Many lighthouses in Ireland are located in areas with abundant marine wildlife. Bring binoculars and keep an eye out for seals, dolphins, and seabirds.
- Take photographs: Lighthouses are often located in picturesque locations, and visiting one can be a great opportunity to take photographs and capture memories of the stunning scenery.
- Enjoy a picnic: Many lighthouses have picnic areas or nearby spots where visitors can enjoy a picnic lunch or snack. Bring a picnic blanket and some food and drink and enjoy a meal with a view.

Visiting a lighthouse in Ireland can be a fun and unique way to experience the local history, architecture, and landscape. Be sure to check the opening hours and any restrictions or safety guidelines in advance, and plan your visit accordingly.

6. Go on a nature hike

If you're looking for ways to spend more time outdoors, a nature hike can be a great option. Not only is it a fun way to spend time together, but it can also help you and your children connect with nature.

If your family has never been on a nature hike before, consider planning one for this summer. There are lots of different types of hikes that your family can try and many of them are free!

Going on a nature hike in Ireland is a fun and healthy activity that can be enjoyed by families. Here are some fun activities you can do while on a nature hike:

- Observe wildlife: Ireland is home to a variety of wildlife, from birds to mammals to insects. Bring a pair of binoculars and observe the animals in their natural habitat. You can also bring a nature guidebook to help identify the species you see.
- Learn about plants and trees: Ireland is known for its lush greenery, and going on a nature hike can be a great opportunity to learn about the different

types of plants and trees that are native to the area. Bring a guidebook or use a nature app to help identify the plants and trees you come across.
- Take photographs: Ireland's natural beauty is stunning, and going on a nature hike can be a great opportunity to capture photographs of the scenery. Bring a camera or use your smartphone to take photos of the flora and fauna you encounter.
- Play nature games: Going on a nature hike can be a fun opportunity to play games with your family.
- Leave no trace: Remember to practice responsible hiking and leave no trace of your visit. This means packing out any trash and respecting the natural environment.

Going on a nature hike in Ireland can be a fun and educational activity for families. Be sure to choose a trail that is suitable for all ages and abilities, and bring appropriate gear like sturdy footwear, hats, sunscreen, and water. With a little planning, a nature hike can be a memorable experience for the whole family.

Chapter 8. Transportation

Public transport in Ireland is generally efficient and well priced. However, it is a good idea to check the route plans for buses and trains before you head out on your trip.

The best way to plan your journey is by downloading the free TFI Journey Planner app or online at Transport for Ireland. It provides door-to-door routes and service information for all licensed public transport providers in Ireland.

Taxi

Taxis in Ireland are a popular and safe way to travel. They're well regulated and offer an alternative to other modes of transport, such as walking or cycling.

The number of taxis in Dublin has increased in recent years, which is partly because of changes to licensing regulations, but also due to the popularity of apps like Uber. Getting a taxi in Ireland is easy and there are many different companies offering services.

In Dublin there are two main types of taxis: licensed and hackney cabs. Licensed taxis are marked by their yellow and blue taxi rooftop sign, while hackney cabs don't have that sign, so it's important to know the difference between them.

Hailing a taxi is fairly simple in Ireland, but you'll need to be sure that the driver has a license. The driver should have a photo on their licence and you can always ask to see it before you get into the car.

If you're looking to book a taxi before you go, there are plenty of websites that let you do that online. There are also many mobile apps that you can download that will show you a list of available cabs and their fares.

A good place to hail a taxi is the North Quays in Dublin's city centre, particularly around Queen Street and O'Connell Street. The queues here are generally fast moving, but can grow at night, so be aware that you may have to wait a little while for a taxi if there's a lot of people in front of you.

You can also find a taxi rank on College Green, just in front of Trinity College and outside the Bank Of Ireland. The queues here are usually shorter during the day, but they can grow considerably after the pubs close.

Once you've hailed a taxi, make sure to tip the driver. It's customary to give them a small percentage of the fare, but don't expect them to refuse a tip.

As with all public transport, it's important to use the National Journey Planner when planning your journey and make sure that you are aware of any changes in service during your trip. This will help you plan the best way to get from point A to B and make sure you arrive on time.

Bus

Many visitors to Ireland think that driving around the country will be the only way they can see the sights, but in fact there are many ways to get around and see the sites without a car. A taxi or a rideshare service like Uber is one option, while another is the bus.

The bus network is spread throughout the whole of the Republic and Northern Ireland, making it a convenient and inexpensive way to travel. Both Bus Eireann and Translink provide a variety of services across the country, from commuter routes to expressways that link major towns.

If you plan on taking the bus, consider buying a Leap Card, which is an electronic card that carries fare money for buses, Luas and DART/commuter rail services. You load the card with a set amount of money and tap it when you board each vehicle, saving you the hassle of carrying cash.

Most major cities have a bus network, including Dublin, Belfast, Cork and Galway. For more information on bus transport in Ireland, visit the Transport for Ireland website.

Buses are an excellent way to explore the countryside and towns, but you should keep in mind that they are not always the fastest way to get there. A good map can help you find your way, and be sure to check the route number that is displayed on the lighted sign on board before leaving.

Cycling

It is also an option in Ireland, especially in urban areas, as it is a low-cost, healthy and environmentally friendly form of transportation. To encourage biking, the government has introduced a tax break for employees who buy new bicycles under the Bike to Work scheme.

Tram

Getting around Ireland by tram is an excellent, and environmentally friendly way to travel. Trams are a quick and convenient alternative to buses or cars, and can also be cheaper than hiring a car.

Dublin's light rail system is known as Luas and has two lines, the Red Line (which connects Saggart and Tallaght with The Point) and the Green Line (which runs from Broombridge northwards to Brides Glen). Since passenger services started in 2004, over 430 million passengers have used the Luas network, and the company is continually expanding the system.

To use Luas, you must have a TFI Leap Card or Valid Pass that is validated at the stop. The TFI Journey Planner App can be used to plan your door-to-door journey on all public transport services in Ireland. The app is available to download for free on your mobile device, and you can buy tickets in advance and travel straight away using the app.

A TFI Leap Card is a reusable smartcard that makes paying for bus, Luas and DART/commuter rail fares more convenient and economical. You can top up the card in stores or online and most fares are discounted when using the card, making it an excellent choice for traveling in Dublin and other Irish cities.

The Red Line has 32 stops and is useful for visitors to get to Jameson Distillery, Collins Barracks (National Museum of Ireland - Decorative Arts & History), Smithfields or Heuston Train Station. It also has a few stops in the city centre including O'Connell Street and Trinity College.

You can transfer between the Red and Green Lines at Abbey Street, O'Connell - GPO and Marlborough Street stops. When you're travelling on the Green Line, you can get off at O'Connell - GPO and walk 2 mins to Abbey Street and board a Red Line tram westbound to Saggart or Tallaght or eastbound to Connolly or The Point.

If you're a tourist and plan to visit the city by tram, it's best to travel on the Red Line for the first part of your trip. The Green Line is not as useful for tourists and you'll need to change trams.

Train

Trains are the most convenient way to travel across Ireland, and are available in both the Republic of Ireland and Northern Ireland. They are run by Iarnrod Eireann in the Republic of Ireland, and by NI Railways in Northern Ireland.

Irish Rail operates InterCity trains between the main cities of Dublin and Cork, while NI Rail operates suburban services. Both run diesel multiple units, known as railcars in Ireland.

The InterCity services use ten 5-car sets, including a 1st Class carriage and a Dining Carriage. They are mainly used on key services between Dublin and Limerick, Galway, Waterford, Westport and Tralee.

There are also twenty-five 4-car sets used on less busy InterCity services, and twenty-eight 3-car sets on lesser used InterCity and commuter routes. These DMUs are operated by IÉ and NIR, with NIR also using the 071 class locomotives for freight services.

Commuter train services are available from Dundalk, Longford and Portlaoise. You can use a Leap Card to purchase fares on these lines and timetables are available from the website of Iarnrod Eireann.

You can get to and from all major towns in Ireland with a train ticket, and the prices are usually much lower than those of buses or taxis. It is recommended that you book your tickets in advance, as they can be up to 50% cheaper than buying them at the station.

If you're a senior citizen, you may be eligible for a discount, or you might qualify for a special SmartPass. These can be bought online or at a train station and are valid on most Irish intercity and local & suburban trains.

There is also a special deal that you can take advantage of called Arrive and Drive which allows you to combine the comfort, convenience and punctuality of a train with the flexibility of a car waiting at your destination.

It is also possible to get a discount on tickets on train tours in Ireland, where you can travel around the country and visit many of its attractions. Purchasing your tickets in advance can save you up to EUR30 per trip.

Maps of attractions

Ireland is a country with rich cultural heritage and beautiful landscapes, and its major cities offer a range of tourist attractions. Let's discuss the maps for the attractions of each major city in Ireland:

Dublin:

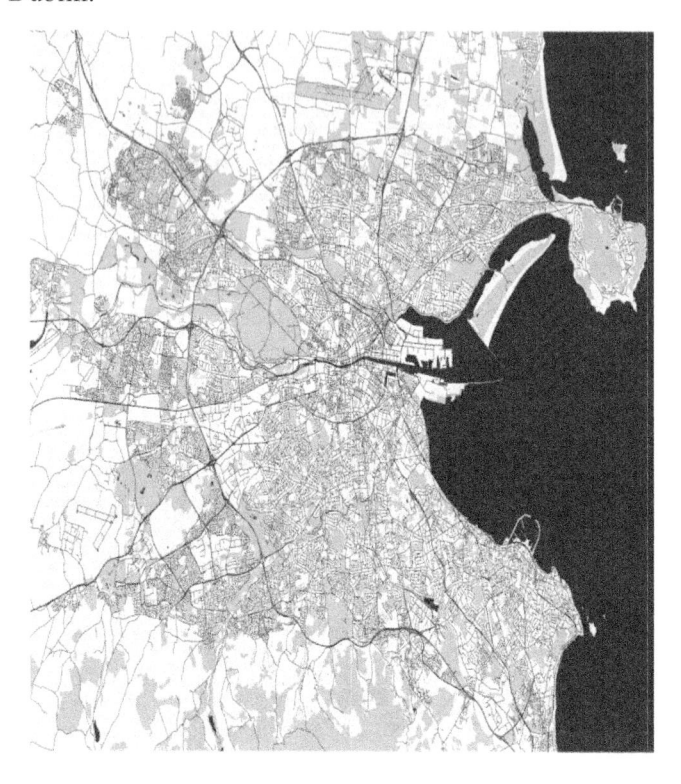

Dublin is the capital city of Ireland, and it has many attractions for tourists. A map of Dublin's tourist attractions would include places such as Trinity College, Guinness Storehouse, Dublin Castle, St. Patrick's Cathedral, Temple Bar, and the National Museum of Ireland. The map should also include the famous Dublin landmarks such as the River Liffey and Ha'penny Bridge.

Cork:

Cork is a city in the south of Ireland and is known for its beautiful waterfront and historic buildings. A map of Cork's tourist attractions would include places such as St. Fin Barre's Cathedral, Cork City Gaol, the English Market, and the famous Blarney Castle. The map should also include the beautiful River Lee and the many parks and gardens in the city.

Galway:

Galway is a city on the west coast of Ireland, and it is known for its beautiful landscapes, traditional music, and lively atmosphere. A map of Galway's tourist attractions would include places such as the Claddagh, Eyre Square, the Spanish Arch, and Galway Cathedral. The map should also include the beautiful Galway Bay and the many walking trails in the area.

Limerick:

Limerick is a city in the mid-west of Ireland, and it is known for its medieval history and cultural heritage. A map of Limerick's tourist attractions would include places such as King John's Castle, the Limerick City Gallery of Art, St. Mary's Cathedral, and the Treaty Stone. The map should also include the beautiful River Shannon and the many historic buildings in the city center.

Waterford:

Waterford is a city in the southeast of Ireland and is known for its Viking heritage and beautiful scenery. A map of Waterford's tourist attractions would include places such as Waterford Crystal, Reginald's Tower, the Bishop's Palace, and the Waterford Greenway. The map should also include the beautiful River Suir and the many walking trails in the area.

Overall, a map of the major cities in Ireland should include the major tourist attractions, landmarks, and natural features of each city. It should be easy to read and follow, and it should be available in different formats, including digital and print, for the convenience of tourists.

Chapter 9.
Seasons to travel

Ireland has a temperate climate and can experience mild, wet winters and cool summers. The best time to visit Ireland is during the summer months of June, July, and August when the weather is typically mild and sunny, and there is less chance of rain. However, it's worth noting that even in the summer, the weather in Ireland can be unpredictable, and it's advisable to pack for all eventualities.

If you're planning to visit Ireland during the spring months of March, April, and May, expect the weather to be chilly with a higher chance of rain. Nevertheless, this is a lovely time to visit Ireland because of the blooming wildflowers and the baby animals in the fields.

During the autumn months of September, October, and November, the weather can be mild, but there's an increasing chance of rain. This is a good time to visit if you're interested in experiencing the colorful fall foliage and seasonal festivals.

If you're planning to visit Ireland during the winter months of December, January, and February, be prepared for wet, chilly weather. However, this is an excellent time to experience Ireland's festive traditions, such as the Christmas markets, and there are fewer tourists.

Packing

When packing for your trip to Ireland, it's essential to consider the weather and activities you plan to undertake. Regardless of the time of year you visit, it's advisable to bring layers of clothing that you can easily add or remove. A waterproof jacket or coat, an umbrella, and waterproof footwear are also essential items to pack as rain is common throughout the year.

Other recommended items to pack include comfortable walking shoes, a hat, and gloves in the colder months, a camera to capture the stunning landscapes, and a power adapter for your electronic devices. Finally, don't forget to bring any necessary medication, travel documents, and travel insurance.

If you plan to explore the countryside, it's advisable to pack clothes suitable for hiking or walking, including comfortable pants or leggings, a long-sleeved shirt, and sturdy walking shoes or boots. It's also worth packing insect repellent if you plan to spend time outdoors.

If you plan to visit some of Ireland's historical sites, such as castles or churches, it's advisable to pack clothing that covers your shoulders and knees, as some of these sites have dress codes.

For those who plan to visit during the summer months, it's worth packing sunscreen, sunglasses, and a sunhat to protect yourself from the sun. It's also worth packing a swimsuit if you plan to swim in the sea or visit a spa.

Overall, when packing for your trip to Ireland, it's essential to consider the weather and the activities you plan to undertake. Bring clothes that are suitable for the season and pack layers that you can easily add or remove depending on the temperature. Finally, don't forget to bring any necessary travel documents, medication, and travel insurance to ensure a smooth and stress-free trip.

Spring

The best way to handle this unpredictable weather is by layering, so be sure to bring a light sweater and a lightweight blazer with you. You can also consider packing one long-sleeved cotton or synthetic-blend button-down shirt with sleeves that can be rolled to the elbow.If you're headed to the beach, a cute sundress is an essential. It's easy to dress up or down and is great for exploring the town during the day and going to a night club in the evening.

Another essential is a pair of comfortable shoes. You can wear sneakers or ankle boots with skirts and dresses, but if you're heading to the beach, make sure you have a pair of sandals as well.

You can also add a pair of shoes with heels, like flats or pumps, for a more formal look. If you're visiting in early spring, pack a pair of sleek waterproof Chelsea boots that look chic with both jeans and dresses.

Norway's spring weather can be chilly, so you'll want to pack plenty of layers. A pair of black trousers and a dark pair of jeans will work, along with a few long-sleeve shirts and sweaters, a blazer or jacket, and a waterproof outerwear piece.

Summer

Whether you're planning to go on a long summer vacation or a short weekend getaway, the right packing plan will help ensure that you arrive in style and ready to enjoy your time away. Having the right packing strategy will also mean less stress and more fun while you're on the road.

During the summer, it's important to pack clothing that is comfortable and light. T-shirts and polo shirts are a great option, especially if you're going to a tropical or beach destination. T-shirts can be paired with lightweight pants or shorts to keep you cool and comfortable throughout the day.

As you prepare to pack for your summer trip, think about the activities that you'll be doing on your vacation and what the weather will be like at those locations. If you'll be spending most of your time outdoors, you may want to bring a pair of hiking shoes or water shoes as well as a bathing suit.

Winter

One of my favorite travel tips for winter is to pack lightweight, functional layers. Layers will allow you to swap out clothes to suit the current conditions and save on luggage space.

Start by choosing base layers that will be versatile enough to wear underneath your other winter clothing, such as long-sleeve t-shirts or thin sweaters. These will occupy less space than thicker jackets or wooly sweaters and they are also easier to wash when you need to refresh them.

Ultimately, winter is the perfect time for you to enjoy a trip with friends and family, and it's worth taking the time to meticulously plan out your wardrobe so you can be comfortable and look your best in each of your destinations. With these tips and a positive attitude, you can have an amazing winter getaway.

Autumn

Autumn in Ireland is a beautiful season, with mild temperatures, colorful foliage, and plenty of cultural events to attend. The season typically runs from September to November, with temperatures ranging from 8°C (46°F) to 14°C (57°F) in September and dropping to 5°C (41°F) to 9°C (48°F) in November.

Here are some items to consider bringing:

- Waterproof jacket: Ireland is known for its rain, so a waterproof jacket is a must-have item.
- Layers: Temperatures can vary throughout the day, so it's a good idea to pack clothes that can be layered.
- Warm sweater: A cozy sweater is essential for chilly evenings.

- Umbrella: Don't forget to pack an umbrella to stay dry during unexpected showers.
- Hat and gloves: As the season progresses, temperatures can drop significantly, so a hat and gloves will come in handy.
- Camera: Autumn in Ireland is stunning, so make sure to bring a camera to capture the beautiful scenery.

In addition to packing appropriate clothing, there are many things to see and do in Ireland during the autumn season. Here are some popular activities:

- Attend a harvest festival: Ireland is famous for its food festivals, and autumn is the time for harvest celebrations.
- Visit a historic site: Ireland has a rich history, and autumn is the perfect time to explore its castles, ancient ruins, and museums.
- Go on a hike: The autumn foliage makes Ireland's landscapes even more breathtaking. There are many hiking trails to explore.
- Attend a music festival: Ireland is known for its traditional music, and many festivals take place in autumn.
- Enjoy a pint of Guinness: A trip to Ireland wouldn't be complete without trying the country's famous stout.

Chapter 10.
The Currency exchange

Currency exchange in Ireland follows the standard practices found in most developed countries. The official currency of Ireland is the Euro (€), which replaced the Irish pound in 2002. The Euro is used by all businesses, banks, and other financial institutions throughout the country.

Foreign currencies can be exchanged for Euros at most banks, foreign exchange bureaus, and post offices. Many hotels and tourist information centers also offer currency exchange services, but their exchange rates may not be as favorable as those found at dedicated currency exchange bureaus.

It is important to note that exchange rates can vary widely depending on the currency being exchanged and the location of the exchange. Rates may also be influenced by fluctuations in global currency markets and political events.

In addition, some businesses in Ireland, particularly those in tourist areas, may accept major foreign currencies such as US dollars or British pounds, but the exchange rate offered may not be favorable. It is generally recommended to use Euros when making purchases in Ireland to avoid any confusion or unnecessary fees.

Overall, currency exchange in Ireland is straightforward and easily accessible, with many options available for travelers to obtain Euros or exchange their foreign currency.

1. Check the Rates Online

If you want to check the currency exchange rates, the best place to start is at your local bank or credit card company. They are likely to have a website that displays rates for different currencies and can often give you better information than other sources.

Some credit cards also offer free foreign ATM withdrawals. However, you should always read the terms and conditions of your card before using it abroad to ensure that you are not charged excessive fees.

One of the most common ways to avoid foreign ATM fees is by choosing a bank that participates in the Global ATM Alliance. This network of large banks waives ATM withdrawal fees for customers who use their card at participating ATMs worldwide.

To find a bank that is part of the Alliance, call your local bank or visit the website. You can also search for a bank that has been approved by the Federal Reserve to be a member of the Alliance.

You should also contact your bank to determine the maximum daily withdrawal limits on your account before leaving for a trip. This will prevent you from having to withdraw more cash than you can afford.

Having a limit will allow you to take out the cash that you need without incurring excessive fees. Some institutions will charge a flat rate or a percentage of the amount withdrawn, but others will also charge a per-transaction fee.

In addition, some ATMs will not dispense receipts, making it hard to know what exchange rate you are paying. In these cases, you can ask to be notified of the exchange rate before you make a withdrawal, and then head directly into a bank to change the currency.

A traveler's best bet for avoiding excessive fees is to use a debit card that charges minimal or no international ATM fees, says Amy Meyers, senior financial counselor at Citibank in New York City. It's also a good idea to contact your bank before your trip to request a higher daily withdrawal limit and to confirm that the fee will be reimbursed.

2. Use a Credit Card

Credit cards are a great way to make purchases and pay them off over time, but they also come with some responsibilities. You need to use them responsibly, keep your card secure and avoid fraudulent activity, both online and in person.

It's best to make sure that you have a credit card with a low interest rate and a long grace period before your payment is due. This will allow you to plan your expenses, and it may also help you avoid overspending or getting into debt.

You should also be aware of the newest features on credit cards, including chip technology. This makes them harder to steal and makes it more difficult for thieves to make fraudulent charges on your account.

Another credit card feature is the ability to file chargebacks. This allows you to dispute a fraudulent transaction and get your money back from the merchant. It's an excellent deterrent to fraudsters, and it can save you from paying for products that aren't worth the price.

This feature is especially useful when traveling abroad. You can easily see the cost of your purchase in local currency and make a smart decision by choosing to pay in the currency you most prefer to use.

If you do opt to pay in your home currency, beware of the dynamic currency conversion rate that some merchants offer. This may sound like a great deal, but it can end up being a big mistake, especially when it comes to foreign transaction fees and overpaying for your purchases.

Finally, you should be aware that some debit cards offer the ability to transfer funds between accounts. This may be helpful when making large purchases or if you need to withdraw cash quickly.

You should always be alert and watch for skimmers, which are magnetic strips or thin devices that can be used to swipe your credit card number. You should freeze your card as soon as you suspect it's been compromised, and contact your bank or credit card company for help acquiring temporary cards or emergency funds.

3. Pay in the Local Currency

One of the best ways to save money and avoid excessive fees while traveling abroad is to pay in the local currency. This will ensure that you are getting a fair exchange rate for your purchases, and it will also help you to avoid dynamic currency conversion (DCC), which is a scam that can result in hefty fees and overpaying for your purchases.

You can also avoid excessive ATM fees by keeping a large amount of cash on hand at all times when traveling abroad. If you need to withdraw cash, be sure to use an ATM that is located inside of a bank rather than on the street, and use it judiciously over a long period of time instead of in small amounts throughout your stay.

Chapter 11.
Irish Dialect Expressions

Ireland is home to a wealth of slang terms and local colloquialisms. Some of them are widely used across the country, while others aren't so well known outside of Ireland.

If you're planning to visit Ireland soon, it may be helpful to brush up on some of these Irish dialect expressions before you arrive. Hopefully you'll be able to get the most out of your trip!

1. Dia duit

From saying hello to ordering a pint of Guinness, there are plenty of slang terms that you may encounter during your time in this beautiful country. Having an understanding of some of the more popular expressions will help you communicate better with Irish people when you visit the Emerald Isle.

This Irish term means a good time, fun, gossip and goings-on. It's one of the most widely used Irish phrases in Ireland and is often heard in social settings such as pubs and bars.

2. The lone wolf

One of those expressions you might hear a lot is the lone wolf. It's a term that originated from wolves, and is used to describe a person that lives on their own without a pack.

This is a sign that you're breaking away from the status quo and doing something your own way, which can be a good thing. However, it's also a sign that you need to take some time to think about what you want and what you don't. Often, people who have a lone wolf personality do better with relationships than others because they value quality over quantity.

3. Look at the state o' you

Craic: This is a popular way of greeting people in Ireland and it means 'fun', 'banter' or 'good times'. It's often used as a response to a question such as 'How are you?'

Culchie: This is another common term for a person who lives in a remote area of Ireland. It's also used to refer to someone who is relatively crafty and can often manipulate situations to benefit themselves.

4. Donkey's years

Donkey's years – While nobody actually knows how long a donkey's year is, the Irish believe it to be a really long time! If you've not seen someone in their 'donkey's years' it means that they haven't been around for several years, even decades. It can also mean that they're just not the same person anymore!

5. Culchie

It is used to describe anyone who lives outside of Dublin. It's a very general term that means someone who isn't from the city and is a little bit different.

Printed in Great Britain
by Amazon